BEAT THE SYSTEM

HOW TO BRIBE MONEY INTO YOUR HAND

JAMES GALLAGHER

The characters and events portrayed in this book are fictitious. Any similarity to real persons, living or dead, is coincidental and not intended by the author.

This book is dedicated first to the Almighty GOD and I want to specially call out my mom for her love and support towards me. I'm also dedicating this book to myself and my mentees for believing in me and that I have what it takes to be among the greats in life.

A piece of top secret information on how to make money passively with very little capital needed.
You first $250 online guaranteed.

MAKE MONEY BOW TO YOU

CONTENTS

"MONEY IS NOT THERE NOR HERE BUT EVERYWHERE"

"Imagine you are financially down at the present time or your pay is minute, the reason is that you either don't have an idea about this reality or you simply don't have the slightest idea where money is or how to acquire it" At that, I wrote this book. You could have just $20 in your pocket at the present time yet when you effectively execute no less than one of the business ideas portrayed in this report, you could be having more than $2000 in the following 30 days. It depends soly upon you. Many will take head while some would just drop it. Many won't download it and miss out. Such a shame!

WHO AM I?

Before we continue, let me rapidly introduce myself on the note *that you don't have any relationship with me. 10years back, I was a broke and baffled individual. I was living on pretty much $500 per month. On numerous days, I made due with just two square meals a day. I needed to be in charge of my pay and live comfortably yet I didn't have any guide and mentor to show me the way. Thus, I began spending my chicken change on books and scanning the web for knowledge. I went through numerous days loaded up with craving, dissatisfaction, and outrage until things began coming into the real world and I began making a decent pay of $3,500 every month From that point, I began putting away more cash to purchase books and projects I could gain from. I began chipping away at the things I was gaining and my pay developed From $3,500 every month to $5,000 per month to $15,000 per month and like that, I have been developing. Not normal for some destitution stricken individuals who have a perpestive limited by fear and hang on firmly to anything they know, I trust in sharing what you know particularly with serious individuals. In this way, I composed a book (presently no longer in production) that is named: "it won't be free"*

The book gives a knowledge into a portion of the things that assisted me with transforming myself into a self-sustainable man.

Be that as it may, in particular, it was an extraordinary motivation to many individuals. I likewise began showing the things I found out about bringing in cash to others by means of classes and different projects. Also, the rare sorts of people who paid attention to me and made a move began getting more cash and expanding the nature of their lives. Some even became tycoons. I could provide you with an extensive rundown of numerous youngsters who are utilizing these organizations to become super wealthy. However, we should leave that for the present and go straight into the fundamental reason for this report. If it's not too much trouble, guarantee that you will put this data to utilize or possibly give it to somebody who will utilize it.

SELLING KNOWLEDGE

I couldn't say whether you have caught wind of selling knowledge previously or your opinion on it. Be that as it may, here is reality. Selling data is a Colossal currency creator that won't dial back at any point in the near future. Why?

The world will keep on getting intricate and individuals will require assist with sorting out a great deal of things. What's more, the great part is that schools can't keep up. Thus, the interest for good and supportive data continues to rise which sets out an enormous freedom for yourself and me. This is the thing I'm attempting to say:

-----No course can teach you social media marketing

-----No course can teach you Multi-Level Marketing

-----No course can teach you how to deal with relationship issues.

-----No course can teach you how to prepare some local or international dishes.

-----No course can teach migration to your dream country

-----No course can teach you Financial freedom or Wealth creation.

Can you see where I am going with this?

Selling data online is what I call - The slow but sure path way to wealth. For instance, you can have just $50 in your wallet at the present time, no business, no worker, no office, but with a valuable information and a good marketing strategy, that $50 could undoubtedly become $500 in a matter of days.

Truth is, I do not even know how much money I have made selling knowledge online. Beginning around 2010 till now, I have researched and gathered knowledge from all most every pillar of life to sell to people. For example, there was a period I sold a report on "How to earn money from paying Taxes".

It was funny at first but I made millions of naira from that. I sold a copy for N1,500 and i sold an average of 10 daily over 4 months. Free feel to do the maths and bear in mind that I was doing this without a business name, office or representative.

YOU DO NOT NEED TO HAVE A PERSONAL EXPERIENCE WITH THE PROBLEM YOUR PRODUCT IS FIXING.

Around 2011, a companion of mine gained admittance to a piece of data about charming a woman. He didn't compose the report. The report was just around 12 pages. He ran a $65 advert in a paper and sold around 50 duplicates at $15 per duplicate the day the advert ran providing him with a moment additional pay of $750 Some other time in 2012, I purchased a report with resale privileges to it for $75. I ran an advert for their port for only $65 out of my $530 or so bank surplus that I had that time. The day the advert ran, I was on a transport en route to Abuja with a companion when the alerts began coming in so quick. One more beneficial thing about selling knowledge (aside from the cash) is the positive feeling you get after knowing you have helped someone in one way or the other. This is presumably why I can't quit selling knowledge. It is likewise presumably why I research in the middle of the night to acquire knowledge and hand it out on a platter of gold for a meagre price.

Now, selling knowldege is very profitable as we have seen. But you need to sell information that is in high demand.
That is what we call a niche.
Your piece of information has to either be solving a problem, or making people feel good about themselves.

Otherwise, it would only be you and rich pitiful person that will purchase your product.. Anything knowledge you are selling must be around 2 things:

(1) It should problem solving.
(2) Or it should ultimately help them reach their goal.

I garauntee you that if your product meets any of those two requirements, then your product would sell.

MOST PROFITABLE NICHES TO SELL KNOWLEDGE ON.

Considering the previous chapter, the largest market for knowledge are under this niches...
---Cash flow
---Health
---Relationship
---Sports

I do not want to bore you with testimonials of people, because It is pointless really.
But if you play your card and target the right leads; There would be no limit to your potential earnings.

Starting a profitbale Knowledge Selling busines is all about 3 stages

(1) Decide on your Niche

(2) Package your product and it must be of high quality

(3)Come up with a solid advertisement strategy

Follow those steps above and you can get started immediately.

Your product can be in any format ranging from

-PDF or Word document

-Video

-Audio

-Course

-Webinar

-Mentorship

AFFILIATE MARKETING

Affiliate Marketing is basically connecting sellers to buyers and earning a comission while doing so. Seems easy right?

Now, there are two ways to go about Affiliate Marketing.

- - - (1) The Strong Offshoot Organizations: These companies are purely affilailiate platforms with tons of affiliates and sellers on it.

Most of them are not free; You will have to pay to get started and they mostly have a yearly membership fee.

Examples are ClickBank, Expertnaire, Digitstem, More Niche, Selar and a lot of others out there

- - - (2) IN-HOUSE Affiliate Networking Project: There are many organizations with in-house subsidiary projects. These projects restrict affiliates to only promote their own products.

Examples are Amazon, Jumia, Konga, Shopify to mention but a few and most of them are free to join but have high targets to be passed for you to get paid. Also, the strong offshoot organizations tend to be more profitbale.

How to get started in The Affiliate Marketing Industry.

1: Sign-up as an affiliate in the platform of your choice.

Be it OffShoot Organizations or In-House projects.

2: Begin by picking one niche (For example technology.) and start a mission to sell an item from that market

3: Begin your mission and get traffic through advertising

campaings.

Now that is easy. All you have to do is advertise, right?

Dead wrong homies.

You have to target your advertisements at the right source or you are just waisting your time and money.

You have to funnel your leads until you get some that are both willing and able to pay.

Then convince them as to why they should buy the product your are affiliating and which they should buy through you.

I have summarized all the qualities a good affiliate has and organized it in a list of four.

(1) They know to select hot niches.

(2) They have a good marketing game and effective advertising campaigns which they use to get lead traffic.

to get a ton of traffic

(3) They are good at Lead Funneling and have a high conversion rate.

(4) They are good at follow up and know how to convince their leads work for them for free.

So check yourself and train yourself to be like the succesful affiliates.

The Affliate Marketing Industry is currently valued at 70 Billion Dollars and it is expected to rise. This is enough proof to show how lucrative it is.

Also, there's no need to fear that the number of affiliates are increasing because an affiliate for a good can be desperate for

another product.
Countless times, I have purchased a product I was affiliating. There would always be sellers and buyers of a product because we humans can never be satisfied.
You just have to search deeper.

IMPORTATION

I bet the first thing that came to your mind is "I do not have money for importation"
Okay, I understand your fears.
Now let me re-phrase it and Call it Mini-Importation and It

revolves around 3 things.
(1) Research on products related to your niche that solves an identified problem.

(2) Buy such items at very cheap countries where cost of production and Labour is cheap and import them in to your country.

(3) Market through advertising campaigns or Affiliates. i

Now, your succes in this business would determine on your niche and the problem it solves.
Also watch out for your import and clearance costs in order to make profits. And better marketing would result to better sales.

The best place to import goods from are China and India. Cost of labour is relatively cheap over there.

There are other sites and I strongly recommend AlliBaba, 1688.
Some products are as cheap as $2 and you could re-sell for about $15.

The secret to earning passively is always having a product to sell and always having someone to sell you.

AMAZON KDP

Amazon Kindle Direct Publishing is another gold mine. But it is literally the hardest because it requires the most work and it is definitely not for everyone, but who am I to judge.

Amazon is hands down one of the largest companies in the world with over 300 million active users.

Now, imagine being on a company where you have over 300 million leads. It is very difficult not to make any sales right?

Now KDP stands for kindle direct publishing. It is all about producing e-books for free and getting paid when your book is bought.

All you have to do is publish a good book then sit back to watch the magic happen.

Now, some people out would tell you that you do not necessarily need writing skills to be success at Amazon KDP. They would bill you and tell you that there's a way to "model" hot selling books. But it is not entirely true. Emphasis on "entirely", but because it works for you does not mean it would work for me.

So my advice is for you to learn.

Acquire writing skills and you would do just fine in Amazon KDP.

One more thing; Be quick.

Amazon KDP is still free at the moment but I do not think it is going to be that way forever.

FOREX AND CRYPTO TRADING.

Trading the international markets are also very profit ONLY IF YOU HAVE LEARNT IT EXTREMELY WELL.

Trading market pairs like AUDUSD, GBPUSD, EURJPY, BTCUSD,BUSDUSD, BTCUSD seem cool and all until it literally drains your source of income and it is best for you to know that it is more addictive that any drug you have heard about.

Before venturing into this profitable but extremely risky business, you would need to learn the nitty gritty of trading and also need to be very disciplined.

You should also note it would most likely take long (could take years) for you to gain mastery of it.

Another way to earn from the crypto space is Crypto mining, crypto remote jobs, crypto arbitrage and crypto staking.
But you would also need to learn them to be profitable from them.

And these businesses are quite capital intensive and also quite expensive to fully learn.

But the profits you would earn would be nothing compared to what you would spend IF YOU GAIN MASTERY OF IT.

CONCLUSION

I have shown you 5 business you could master and financially liberate yourself.

- Selling Knowledge
-Affiliate Marketing
-Importation
-Amazon KDP
-Forex and Crypto Trading

All you have to do is choose one and learn it; pay for courses on; then start earning from it.

ABOUT THE AUTHOR

James Gallagher

A young entrepreneur that has cracked the secrets to bribing money. James Gallagher has learned the nitty gritty of making money online and he is now selling this priceless piece of information for a token.

The Ultimate Joker Card To Wealth

www.ingramcontent.com/pod-product-compliance
Lightning Source LLC
LaVergne TN
LVHW052113160826
845678LV00015B/3536

* 9 7 9 8 3 5 6 9 1 2 9 2 4 *